GARDEN RO

COASTAL SPLEND

1

THE OVERBERG AND SWELLENDAM

The Overberg (1), regarded as the western gateway to the Garden Route, is South Africa's garden of plenty, rich in wheat and barley, fruit and flowers, cattle and sheep. To the earliest settlers, it was a far-off place, reached by crossing the 'Mountains of Africa'. Today it is just one hour's drive from Cape Town. It has many attractions for the traveller, most notably the meeting point of the Atlantic and Indian oceans, on a jagged beach at Cape Agulhas. History lives in a dozen or so tiny mission towns and fishing villages, several of which are preserved in their entirety as National Monuments. And along the coastline, whales mate and calve from June to December each year.

Gracious Swellendam combines culture with agriculture, history with nature. The town lies at the foot of the Langeberg range, and is overlooked by the Marloth Nature Reserve. Swellendam's Drostdy (2), just one of the town's architectural treasures, was built in 1746, and is now the centrepiece of an important museum complex reflecting village and farm life in

2

4

old South Africa. South of the town is the Bontebok National Park with its small, protected population of these unusually marked and once almost extinct antelope (3). Situated on the banks of the Breede River, the park is in a rich coastal fynbos zone, with around 500 plant and grass species. Closer to the coast, the mouth of the Gourits River is spanned by the 61-metre-high Gourits River Bridge which has become a launching pad for bungee-jumpers (4) who congregate there regularly for local and national events. Once the highest bridge in South Africa, it stretches more than 200 metres across the gorge and carries the main Garden Route highway, the N2, over the gap.

3

5

6

7

MOSSEL BAY

Mossel Bay is one of two large, well-defined bays on the Garden Route; the other is Plettenberg Bay to the east. The resorts which have developed around these havens are among the most desirable Garden Route destinations, with mild weather, safe bathing and clean, sandy beaches (8). Once an important export harbour, Mossel Bay remains a major port (10) but is today best known for leisure pursuits. The bay is a base for helicopter flips and short cruises to Seal Island, and shelters the large yacht basin tucked into its eastern curve (5). It was here that Bartolomeu Dias landed in 1488 after bypassing the

8

9

10

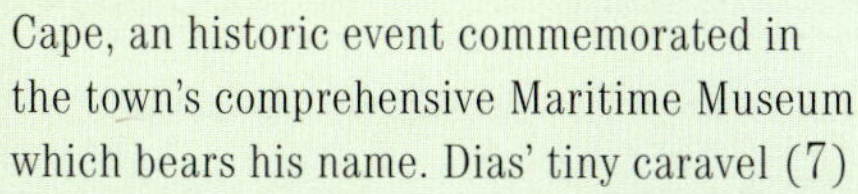

Cape, an historic event commemorated in the town's comprehensive Maritime Museum which bears his name. Dias' tiny caravel (7) is replicated in the museum; it was in this very craft that the brave journey was re-enacted five centuries later, in 1987. A glowing stained glass window in the museum (6) reminds us of Portugal's early claim to the area with a *padrão*, or stone cross, planted in a prominent position; a replica has been raised on the actual site nearby. Early seafarers left messages for passing ships in a large milkwood tree (9), reputedly the same one standing today; a small stream which supplied the sailors with fresh water still flows past the tree, and visitors can mail postcards from a box at the 'Post Office Tree'. A fascinating variety of shells (11) are displayed in an annexe to the large stone building which houses the Bartolomeu Dias Museum, a Local History Museum and an Information Centre.

11

12

13

GREAT BRAK RIVER AND ROBINSON PASS

Twin rivers, rising in the mountain ranges alongside the Garden Route, create tranquil lagoons and estuaries where they meet the sea east of Mossel Bay. Great Brak River (12 and 13) and its Little Brak sibling, thread between forested hills and serene beaches, creating an idyllic setting for holiday homes. A lush backdrop is provided by the Jonkersberg north of Great Brak; these mountains are part of the Outeniqua range which separates the narrow coastal terrace from the Little Karoo. The great engineer Thomas Bain built the Robinson Pass through the Jonkersberg in 1869, and today's visitor can drive through spectacular mountain vegetation along this historic route (15). The summit of the pass is over 800 metres high, and gives far-reaching

15

14

mountain and ocean views. Most of the upper slopes on the sea-facing side are under cover of coastal fynbos and stands of forest, with proteaceous plants dominant. The *Protea aristata*, or Ladismith sugarbush (16), is one of South Africa's best-loved and most striking blooms.

Aside from a few scattered farms and Eight Bells Holiday Farm, a mountain resort at the foot of the pass, the area is sparsely inhabited. Outrides from the resort allow guests a closer look (14) at the rich vegetation and scenery, while two interesting trails take hikers either to the Ruitersbos State Forest on the eastern side of the pass, or on the western Koumashoek Circuit. A third – the Attaquaskloof Pass – links the Robinson Pass with the earliest chapter of the history of the region. It was here, in 1689, that the first Europeans crossed the Outeniquas with the help of Khoi-khoi guides of the resident Attaqua tribe.

16

18

17

19

GEORGE AND SURROUNDS

Although the N2 highway gives travellers the option of by-passing George, it shouldn't be missed by any serious explorers of the Garden Route. After all, the 18th century naturalist François le Vaillant described it as 'the most beautiful land in the universe'. George is an undeniably pretty place with broad streets and great old oak trees. The Outeniqua Mountains tower behind the town, agricultural fields and downs lie at its fringes, it boasts the most prestigious golf course in the country, and several lovely beaches are within a 15-minute drive. Justifiably, George is named the capital of the Garden Route. Set in a beautiful garden with blue agapanthus, the Dutch Reformed Church (17) is an imposing landmark in the town. The tiny stone St Marks Anglican Cathedral (19) – the smallest cathedral in the southern hemisphere – confers city status on George. The high annual rainfall creates near-perfect turf for the golf courses, including the luxurious Fancourt Hotel and Country

0

21

Club Estate (18), which have brought international renown to this small city. The approach to Herolds Bay (20) is via a steep road through coastal dunes which reveals the sea as a spectacular surprise at the final bend. The Outeniqua Pass (22) is a major link between the coast and the Little Karoo. Its southern and northern faces display two entirely different vegetation types, of the coastal and semi-arid zones. Although not for amateurs, a walk up 1 337-metre-high George Peak may reveal the rare and protected *Cyrtanthus elatus*, or George lily (21), which flowers only in March and after fire.

22

23

24

LITTLE KAROO AND OUDTSHOORN

Beyond the coastal terrace and over the mountains, the land is swiftly transformed from green abundance to semi-arid scrubland. Most of the plants, such as the indigenous mountain aloe (*Aloe arborescens*) (25), have intricate survival mechanisms to store water and prevent evaporation. Despite its barren appearance, the Little Karoo, and even the Great Karoo beyond the next mountain barrier, is surprisingly fertile. Infrequent rain means that

25

26

27

the soil is not leached of valuable nutrients, and all it takes is water to produce the sun-ripened fruit, tobacco and lucerne, for which the Cango Valley is known.

The Little Karoo's most valuable harvest, however, is feathers – those of the prehistoric, flightless bird, distant relative of the dinosaur, the ostrich. This lightweight harvest was worth its weight in gold during the turn-of-the-century feather boom. Ostrich farming (23) is still heavily concentrated in the Cango Valley around Oudtshoorn and De Rust, but now it is the meat and hides that command the highest prices.

The pretty hamlet of De Rust lies at the entrance to Meiringspoort, a spectacularly scenic river gorge which runs through the mighty Swartberg mountains at the tip of the Great Karoo. A feathery waterfall (24) plunges down near-vertical cliffs into the Groot River in the heart of the gorge. The legendary wealth of the ostrich barons lives on in Oudtshoorn's 'feather palaces', fanciful stone mansions with elaborate ornamentation, and many, such as Welgeluk (26), are National Monuments. Ostriches share domestic duties (27) the dun-feathered female guarding the eggs by day, while her mate sits at night, well-camouflaged by his black feathers. Ostriches are the fastest birds on earth, and can reach incredible speeds of up to 48 kilometres per hour.

28

29

30

OUDTSHOORN AND CANGO CAVES

The dominant feature on the landscape is the majestic Swartberg range which separates the Little (32) and Great Karoo. Once an impenetrable barrier, the mountain can now be breached via three 'gateways', providing some of the country's most breathtaking scenery. Considered one of the great road passes of southern Africa, the Swartberg Pass (28) winds through a series of dizzying hairpin bends and fabulous views to the 1 585-metre-high summit. Access is either from the historical hamlet of Prince Albert, which lies at its feet on the northern face, or from Oudtshoorn in the south. Thirty kilometres outside of Oudtshoorn, at the foot of the Swartberg Pass, the Cango Caves burrow deep into the heart of the mountains in a series of chambers and labyrinths as yet not fully explored. The Cango Caves – one of South Africa's most popular tourist attractions – are among the world's finest dripstone caves, and the Van Zyl Hall (31) is named for the farmer who discovered the caves. On the outskirts of town, the Cango Crocodile ranch is home to an interesting collection of animals which includes more than 400 crocodiles (30) and alligators of all ages and sizes. The park incorporates a cheetah farm, with a 'catwalk' over the enclosures, and the option of 'hugging a cheetah' (29) for a fee donated to conservation.

31

32

34

33

35

KAAIMANS RIVER AND VICTORIA BAY

An old-established holiday home sits in splendid isolation on the far bank of the Kaaiman's River (33) near its estuary at the Wilderness. The peat-stained water is so dark as to be almost black, and when calm, reflects a perfect mirror-image of the densely forested headland. Like Herolds Bay, Victoria Bay was established almost 100 years ago; the tiny sheltered bay creates perfect surfing waves (34) and is a favoured spot for family holidays (35). 'Vic Bay', as it is affectionately known, is halfway between George and the Wilderness. By hopping on board the Outeniqua Choo-Tjoe, a vintage steam train that crosses the Kaaiman's River mouth (36) via a graceful rail bridge, travellers enjoy a bird's-eye view of one of the most beautiful sights along the Garden Route. Drawn by a Class 24 steam engine, the train travels daily between George and Knysna carrying passengers on a scenic three-hour ride and shuttling necessary goods between the towns.

36

37

38

WILDERNESS LAKES AREA

The earth's movement over the ages has created a series of lakes which run parallel to the sea along the southern Cape coast. The lakes are 'drowned' river valleys and basins, separated from the sea by dunes of varying geological ages and which have become stabilised by sedimentation and vegetation. Among them is the highest vegetated dune in South Africa which provides a 200-metre backdrop to Groenvlei, also known as Lake Pleasant. Dune vegetation is composed mainly of relatively young fynbos plant communities and small herbs, many of which have waxy leaves to provide resistance to salt-laden sea air. The lakes and dunes have together created one of South Africa's most scenic regions. The westernmost Island Lake (37) is fed by the Touw River, via the winding Serpentine Channel, and the Duiwe River, two of many rivers which have their source in the Outeniqua Mountains.

39

40

41

Groenvlei (38) lies further east with its southern shore inside the boundaries of the Goukamma Nature Reserve, adjoining the Wilderness National Park. The only freshwater lake in the system, Groenvlei has been stocked with bass and offers excellent fishing (42). Although leisure activities – such as sailing, hiking and skiing – are welcomed throughout the Wilderness National Park, water-skiing is limited to Island Lake and Swartvlei. Several resorts lie within the boundaries of the park, offering good facilities and affordable accommodation, including caravan and camp sites. The Fairy Knowe Hotel (41), and the Lakes Resort (40) which provides sailboards and canoes for visitors, is on the banks of the Touw River on the western fringe of the national park. Throughout the park and the adjoining reserves, walks and hikes show off the wealth of birds, plants and animals of the forests, lakes and intertidal zone. The rich birdlife includes the Knysna loerie and several kingfisher species, including the black and white pied kingfisher (*Ceryl rudis*) (39), and there are carefully situated bird hides at Rondevlei and Bo-Langvlei.

42

43

44

45

KNYSNA AND BELVIDERE

Knysna was once home to woodcutters and whalers but is now a teeming holiday town with property prices to match its popularity. Set in an environment rich in forests and mountains, the town tumbles down to the banks of the 17-square-kilometre Knysna Lagoon (43), a focal point for seafood restaurants (48), recreational

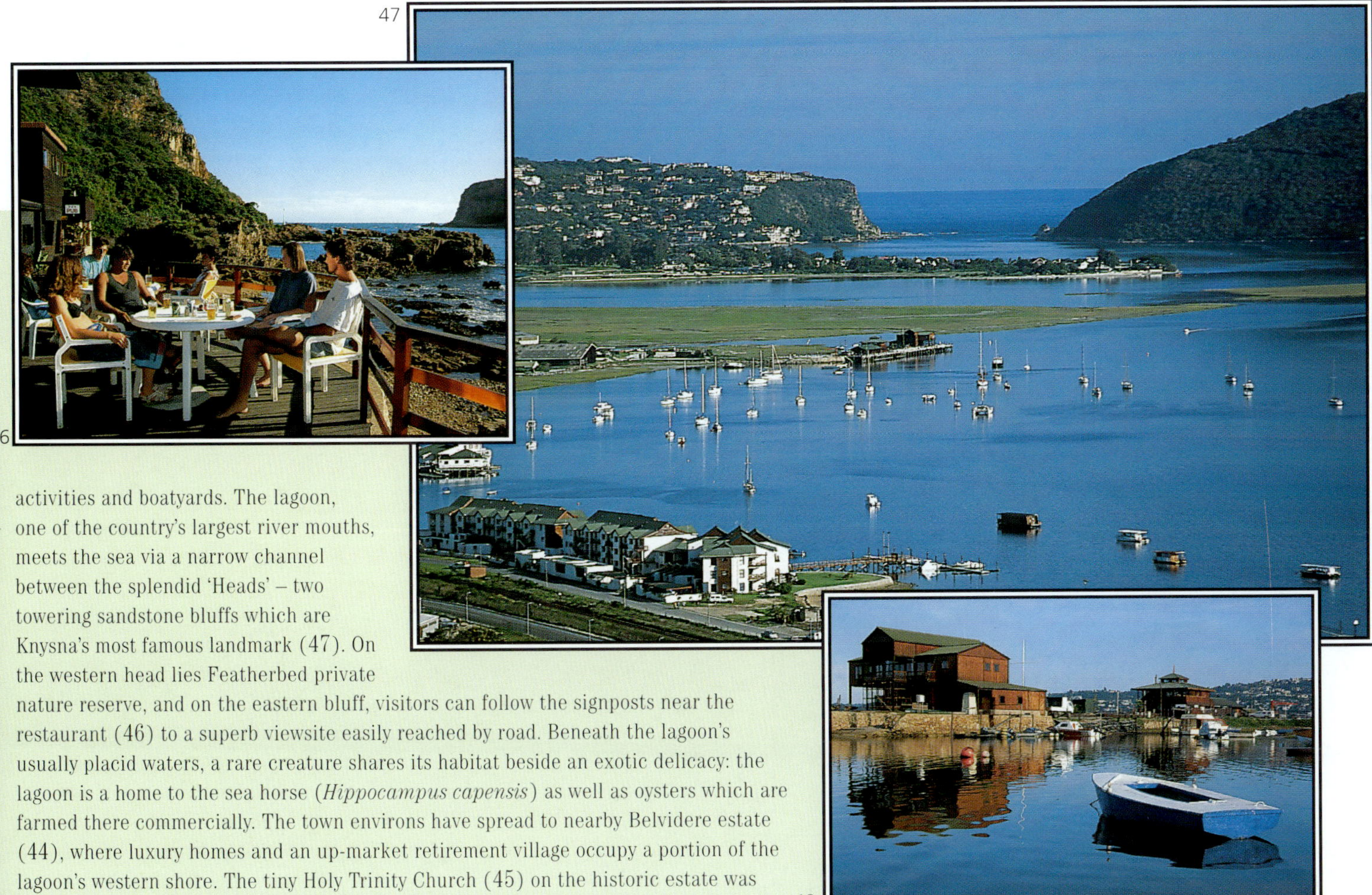

47

46

activities and boatyards. The lagoon, one of the country's largest river mouths, meets the sea via a narrow channel between the splendid 'Heads' – two towering sandstone bluffs which are Knysna's most famous landmark (47). On the western head lies Featherbed private nature reserve, and on the eastern bluff, visitors can follow the signposts near the restaurant (46) to a superb viewsite easily reached by road. Beneath the lagoon's usually placid waters, a rare creature shares its habitat beside an exotic delicacy: the lagoon is a home to the sea horse (*Hippocampus capensis*) as well as oysters which are farmed there commercially. The town environs have spread to nearby Belvidere estate (44), where luxury homes and an up-market retirement village occupy a portion of the lagoon's western shore. The tiny Holy Trinity Church (45) on the historic estate was built in the style of an 11th-century Norman church and consecrated for use in 1855.

48

49

50

51

KNYSNA TOWN AND ENVIRONS

After a century or so as a woodcutters' and fishermen's village, Knysna's identity as a travel destination has emerged only in the last decade or two. Today the town has a sophisticated infrastructure geared towards tourism, which spills over into the surrounding districts. The N2 highway, for easily 50 kilometres east and west of the town, has become a recognised tourist route with B&B accommodation, farmstalls, craft shops, furniture outlets and roadside vendors plying their trade cheek by jowl. It has also become a destination for major annual sporting events, such as the Head to Head marathon (51), each of which attracts thousands of visitors to the town. A farmstall on the fringes of the Knysna Forest (49) is named for one of the popular walks through the dense forests; there are three well-signposted Elephant Walks, but one is unlikely to encounter the last of the remaining four-footed giants.

52

53

54

Knysna's sophisticated shopping mall in the town centre offers beautifully crafted birds, dolphins, lamps and other artefacts made of indigenous woods (52). The mall has been built in an appealing country village style to complement its surroundings, and incorporates a number of pavement cafés and bistros (50). Informal traders, too, have their day, with the advantage of mobility to be where the action is (53). Noetzie, a secluded cove west of Knysna, is accessible only via a steep footpath. The beautiful beach is overlooked by a number of brooding sandstone 'castles' (54), the holiday homes of several Zimbabwean families.

55

56

57

KNYSNA FOREST

Deep in the brooding forests skirting Knysna, the relics of a tiny mining settlement recall a brief gold rush in the 1880s. Millwood House (56), one of the original houses in the mining village, has been restored and moved to Knysna. The Knysna Museum houses a fascinating photographic history of the mining activities, which includes the alluvial fields at Jubilee Creek (55), now enjoyed as a park and picnic site incorporating meadow, forest and stream. The sights, sounds and rich smells of the forest are best appreciated by following the walking trails, most of which require only light exertion and leave ample time to enjoy the bird calls, paddle in the gentle streams and gaze at the towering height of the dense forest canopy. For more serious hikers a two-day coastal trail starts in the Harkerville Forest (59) and traverses 26,5 kilometres.

59

8

The most common forest tree today is the ironwood (*Olea capensis*), and the famed Big Tree (57) in the Garden of Eden is an Outeniqua yellowwood (*Podocarpus falcatus*), seven metres in diameter and reaching a height of 46 metres. It stands in a small clearing about 350 metres from the highway and is reputed to be 800 years old.

The fertile forest floor yields its own riches of ferns, mosses and fungi which glow as bright as flowers (58). But the king of the forest is Knysna's endemic bird, the loerie (*Tauraco corythaix*) (60). Boldly crested and coloured, its call is just as brazen, and many a hiker has been startled by its raucous cry tearing through the still, cool depths. Although sometimes difficult to detect in the thick forest growth, the loerie's bright red underwings are easily visible in flight.

60

61

63

62

PLETTENBERG BAY AND ROBBERG

Plettenberg Bay is the glamour capital of the Garden Route, and like Mossel Bay, development is centred around a large, sheltered bay. Variously known in days gone by as the Bay of Beauty and the Bay of Content, today it is simply called 'Plett'. The waters are warm and serene, and lagoons edge lazily onto immense white, sandy beaches with a backdrop of lavishly vegetated dunes. The air's ozone content is almost tangible, giving Plett a bracing fragrance that imparts an instant sense of well-being. From the small hilltop village centre, the road sweeps down to the sea, culminating in a picturesque promontory flanked by Central and Robberg beaches.

64

Occupying a spectacular position, the Beacon Island resort hotel (64) is at the tip of the promontory where a whaling station once stood. The hotel's swimming pool (65) is set in lawns at the water's edge; when guests are not using the pool, seagulls are quick to take over. Robberg Beach terminates in a 4-kilometre-long peninsula (61) where seals, whales and dolphins can be spotted from several sites along a circular walk. A cave on the western face houses a midden, with Stone Age tools and artefacts. Among the shells found by the early inhabitants would have been the delicate pansy shell (*Echinodiscus bisperforatus*), emblem of Plettenberg Bay, which is a prized trophy for today's shell-seekers (62). Hobie Beach (63) is a focal point for watersports which are enjoyed year-round in Plettenberg Bay.

65

66

67

KEURBOOMS RIVER AREA

A few kilometres east of Plettenberg Bay, the confluence of the Bietou and Keurbooms rivers creates a broad, lagoon-like estuary. Several riverside resorts have been developed along its banks, providing holidaymakers with the perfect base to explore the river reaches, to fish, swim, sail, ski and – at nearby Keurboomstrand – to surf. Arch Rock (66) is a well-known landmark on the beach and end-point of the Wittedrift School Trail which hugs the shoreline. The Keurbooms River Nature Reserve covers a hilly plateau overlooking the Keurbooms River and its upper reaches (67), where motorised dinghies and skiing are permitted. Visitors can explore the river and reserve by canoe, with an overnight stop at a 12-person hut, or take a one-hour hike through coastal fynbos along the river banks. Within the reserve lies one of the oldest-established public resorts on the river (68), with chalets, camping, picnic and caravanning facilities under a canopy of trees at the water's edge.

69

71

70

NATURE'S VALLEY

One of South Africa's most acclaimed hikes, the Otter Trail ends in lovely Nature's Valley (69). The little settlement on the floodplain of the Groot River is part of the De Vasselot reserve area at the western edge of the Tsitsikamma National Park which stretches for 65 kilometres between Nature's Valley and Oubosstrand to the east. The De Vasselot section, a 2 500-hectare natural collage of forested valley, river mouth, floodplain and lagoon, also protects large areas of vulnerable coastal plateau fynbos. Many of the hikes and trails in the area reward hikers with a sensational view of the Salt River mouth (71), west of Nature's Valley. The river mouth can also be reached via a coastal walk at

72

73

low tide. Unlike many other coastal developments, Nature's Valley has its own style of architecture sympathetic to the national park, and houses are generally of wood, tucked under a dense cover of vegetation (70). It is not unusual to have forest-dwelling vervet monkeys (73) scampering over the roofs or playing in the trees overhead. Visitors travelling by road can take the toll highway spanning three spectacular gorges via road bridges such as this one at Bloukrans (72), the longest single-span concrete bridge in the world. An alternative scenic route is the old road through the Bloukrans and Groot River passes, which plunges into the heart of the gorge, winding through walls of dense vegetation.

74

75

76

STORMS RIVER

After its serene passage towards the Indian Ocean, the Storms River meets the sea in a dramatic setting of sheer cliffs and roaring surf (74). At Skietklip (75), waves pound the jagged rocks, creating towering walls of spray and providing a never-ending drama for the many visitors who come here to hike, camp or simply to contemplate nature's wonders. The National Parks Board rest camp at Storms River is world-renowned and provides comprehensive information, accommodation and a landmark for the many trails that start or end here.

78

77

The Otter Trail begins at the rest camp and within 2,5 kilometres takes walkers to the waterfall (76) which cascades in an elegant series of ledges to a deep brown pool – a typical habitat for the clawless Cape Otter (77) which, although rarely seen, gives its name to the trail. This part of the walk is open to the public, and offers a taste of what's to come on the five-day hike west to Nature's Valley. The Mouth Trail east of the camp crosses a swaying suspension bridge (79) over the river and gives glimpses of the river's earlier passage down the quiet gorge; from the end of the bridge, the fit and not-so-fit can decide whether to descend to one of a number of small rocky bays, or continue a steep climb to the eastern bluff (78) to take in sweeping views of the river mouth and rest camp beyond.

79

80

BLOUKRANS AND GROOT RIVER PASSES

The Tsitsikamma Forest was once so dense as to be considered impenetrable until a devastating fire in 1869 cleared the way, and the road through the Bloukrans and Groot River (80) passes was completed in 1884 by famed engineer Thomas Bain. Although the plateau was almost denuded by the fire, the river gorges still retain deep stands of indigenous vegetation. The immense height and age of the trees rising from the slopes and the valley floors create a breathtaking spectacle.